LEVEL 2 READER

SAFARI BABIES

by
Joan Emerson

Scholastic Inc.

PHOTO CREDITS:

Cover: cheetah: Villiers Steyn/Shutterstock; sign: enviromantic/iStockphoto; back cover: Suzi Eszterhas/Minden Pictures; bark and leaf patterns throughout: cgtextures; p. 1: cheetah: Villiers Steyn/Shutterstock; sign: enviromantic/iStockphoto; p. 3: nstanev/iStockphoto; p. 5: Snowleopard1/iStockphoto; p. 6: Suzi Eszterhas/Minden Pictures; p. 9: ratluk/iStockphoto; p. 10: laytonjeff/iStockphoto; p. 13: Philip Perry/Minden Pictures; p. 14: abxyz/Shutterstock; p. 17: ZSSD/Minden Pictures; p. 18: McDonald Wildlife Photog./Animals Animals; p. 21: namibelephant/iStockphoto; p. 22: Hedrus/Shutterstock; p. 25: Villiers Steyn/Shutterstock; p. 26: Art Morris/Visuals Unlimited/Getty Images; p. 29: Anup Shah/Animals Animals; p. 30: pjmalsbury/iStockphoto.

ISBN 978-0-545-72460-9

12 11 10 9 8 7 6 5 4 3 2 1 14 15 16 17 18 19

Printed in China 68
First printing, September 2014

Designer: Marissa Asuncion
Photo Editor: Cynthia Carris

INTRODUCTION

Lions and leopards and hippos, oh my! The African wilderness is home to some of the most adorable animal babies in the world. Africa is a huge **continent**. It is so big that the United States could fit inside of it three times! Not all of Africa looks the same. Many different kinds of animals can be found there. If you can't take a trip to the African wilderness, don't worry! Just flip the page to come face-to-face with your favorite safari babies!

LION

A female lion, called a lioness, gives birth to one to six lion cubs at a time. Lions live in a big family called a **pride**. Each pride is made up of fifteen to forty lions. Together, the pride eats, sleeps, raises their cubs, and defends their home. When lion cubs are about one year old, they start helping with pride duties—like hunting.

A lion's roar can be heard five miles away!

GORILLA

Adult gorillas are known for their long, thick coats of hair—but they don't start out that way! At birth, baby gorillas are nearly hairless. As they grow, so does their hair! At eight weeks old, baby gorillas begin to smile, laugh, and play.

Gorillas can learn sign language!

AFRICAN ELEPHANT

African elephants have long floppy ears that are shaped like the continent of Africa! At birth, the babies, called calves, weigh more than an average adult human. They can grow to weigh as much as 14,000 pounds. That's as heavy as a school bus! A calf uses its long nose, called a **trunk**, to smell, breathe, drink, grab things, and even make noise.

Elephants use their trunks like snorkels when they swim.

GIRAFFE

Giraffes are known for their long necks and long legs. A full-grown giraffe is so tall it can look into a two-story window just by standing! Baby giraffes, called calves, learn to use their necks and legs quickly. They are usually born around six feet tall, and can run and eat leaves in just one day!

Giraffes sleep only twenty to thirty minutes a day!

AFRICAN LEOPARD

African leopards are closely related to lions. As babies, leopards even look like lion cubs. But unlike lions, African leopards are **solitary** animals, meaning they like to live alone. Around two years old, these leopards leave their mothers and begin to live on their own.

A leopard's tail can be as long as its entire body!

Baby hippos, called calves, weigh about ten times more than human babies. Calves are born in rivers and spend much of their lives there. Still, hippos cannot swim! Instead, they push off of the bottom and sides of rivers and **gallop** to where they want to go. That's how they earned the name hippopotamus, which means "river horse."

A hippo's closest relatives are whales and dolphins!

HEDGEHOG

Hedgehogs are famous for their spiky hair, called quills. On average, an adult hedgehog has over 6,000 quills. Baby hedgehogs are called hoglets or piglets. When a hoglet is born, it is pink, blind, and has soft white quills. Within one day, the hoglet sheds its soft quills and grows 150 spiky ones!

A hedgehog's quills are home to as many as 500 fleas!

NILE CROCODILE

Before it is born, a baby Nile crocodile is so small that it fits into a four-inch egg. When it's ready to hatch, the mother or father crocodile rolls the egg between its tongue and the top of its mouth to help the baby crack out of the shell. The baby crocodile grows and grows and grows. An adult can weigh up to 2,000 pounds!

A Nile crocodile's stomach can hold ten pounds of rocks, which they swallow to help with digestion.

AFRICAN RHINOCEROS

An African rhinoceros has two horns that grow from its head. A mother uses these horns for protection. A father uses them to battle **predators**. A baby rhinoceros, called a calf, is born without horns. Each year, its horns grow about three inches. Its longest horn can grow up to five feet!

Rhinos have lived on Earth for more than 50 million years!

JACKAL

Jackal babies, called pups, are born blind. They learn to see in just one to two weeks. Even with sight, pups need a lot of care. Older siblings help their parents look after the young pups. They live together as a family either underground in a **den** or in a cave.

Jackals yell, yap, and howl to communicate with each other.

CHEETAH

The cheetah is the fastest animal on Earth. But when a cheetah is born, it cannot even crawl! It's not until a cheetah cub is eight months old that it begins to run. Even then, it takes practice for it to sprint at top speed. Fully grown cheetahs can go from zero to seventy miles per hour in two seconds. That's quicker than the fastest car in the world!

**Cheetahs do not roar—
they purr like housecats!**

AFRICAN BUFFALO

With its sharp horns and heavy weight, the African buffalo is one of the strongest creatures in the wild. Females live in **herds** of up to 1,000 buffalo. When traveling, the newborn calves walk in the middle of the herd for protection. Soon, the calves grow their own horns and are able to defend themselves against predators.

African buffalo are also called Cape buffalo, since they live in the Cape of Good Hope, South Africa.

OSTRICH

Ostriches are birds that cannot fly. They are the largest and heaviest birds in the world. So it makes sense that they also lay the biggest eggs. Ostrich eggs weigh three pounds. Like other birds, ostrich **chicks** hatch from eggs. Since they cannot fly, ostriches make nests on the ground instead of in trees.

Ostriches can live for up to fifty years!

ZEBRA

Zebras are members of the horse family. And just like horses, zebras live in herds, males are called stallions, and babies are called **foals**. Zebras are known for their black and white stripes. These stripes make it hard for predators to pick out one zebra from the herd. Foals are born with brown and white stripes that turn darker as they get older.

No two zebras' stripes are alike!

GLOSSARY

chick: a very young bird

continent: one of the seven large landmasses on Earth. The continents are Asia, Africa, Europe, North America, South America, Australia, and Antarctica

den: the home of a wild animal

digestion: the process of breaking down food so that it can be absorbed into the blood and used by the body

foal: a young horse, mule, donkey, or zebra

gallop: to run quickly with all four feet off the ground at once

herd: a large number of animals that live together or move together

predator: an animal that lives by hunting other animals for food

pride: a group of lions

solitary: living alone without depending on others

trunk: an elephant's long nose